Books are to be returned on or before
the last date below.

T   ucts

LIBREX–

Evans

D1357531

Contents

Introduction

Since humans began using wood to make fire, timber has been one of the most important resources on Earth. It is used as a fuel, in building construction, and to make furniture and paper. Its versatility has resulted in widespread destruction of woodland and forest areas, and now this precious resource is threatened. The dangers of continued deforestation have been recognised, however, and governments and organisations in many parts of the world have taken steps to manage the use of timber sustainably.

There are two types of timber – hardwoods and softwoods. Hardwood trees have pores (tiny holes) in their trunks and softwood trees do not. Softwood trees include conifers such as the Douglas fir and pine, and they are easy to cut and work with. Softwood timber has a range of uses – paper, frames for buildings and windows, doors, staircases, MDF and chipboard, as well as furniture. Hardwood trees have broad, flat leaves and enclosed nuts or seeds, and include oak, ash and walnut. Hardwood timber is also good for construction, as it is more weather-resistant than softwood, but it is also more expensive and difficult to work with. Hardwoods are often used for flooring, doors and furniture. There are 100 times more hardwood species than softwood.

Forest Types

Hardwoods and softwoods are found in six types of forest area on Earth: tropical rainforest, tropical

These logs are being transported, having been cut from a hardwood forest in Gabon. Forestry and wood export is an important part of the economy of this West African country.

monsoon forest, Mediterranean forest, temperate evergreen forest, temperate deciduous forest and coniferous forest. Not all of these provide sources of timber for use in everyday life, though, and large-scale timber use is mainly focused on tropical rainforest, temperate deciduous forest and coniferous forest.

Tropical rainforest is the world's most important environment. It is home to many unique plants and animals, and plays a part in balancing Earth's climate. Tropical rainforest can be found stretching around the world between the Tropics of Cancer and Capricorn, north and south of the Equator. In these areas, the temperature is consistently high (around 27°C) and there is a lot of rainfall.

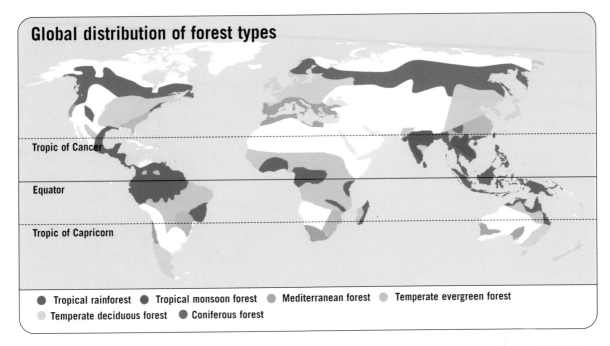

Global distribution of forest types

Tropic of Cancer

Equator

Tropic of Capricorn

● Tropical rainforest ● Tropical monsoon forest ● Mediterranean forest ● Temperate evergreen forest
● Temperate deciduous forest ● Coniferous forest

Temperate deciduous forest lies in the temperate zones, between 30° and 50° degrees north and south of the Equator. This type of forest can also be found on the west coast of Europe as far north as Norway.

Coniferous forest, also called taiga or boreal forest, is only found in mountainous areas in the southern hemisphere. It is more common on the northern continents of North America, Europe and Asia.

Exploitation or Sustainability?

Timber is the raw material for many essential items used all over the world. In some less economically developed countries (LEDCs) it is the main energy source. Because it is so valuable, timber will inevitably continue to be used. Although deforestation has become widespread, the benefit of wood is that it is a renewable resource. Unlike coal or oil, for example, new trees can always be planted, and they do not take millions of years to grow. However, in some places trees are still being cut down at a faster rate than new trees are being grown, and careful management is needed to ensure a sustainable future for timber use.

This area of forest in Washington, USA, is being 'clearcut' – a technique in which all the trees in an area are cut down at the same time.

FACTS IN FOCUS
Saving the Rainforest?

It is a common belief that saving or recycling paper 'saves the rainforest'. In fact, this is not strictly true. Rainforests are largely made up of hardwoods, and very few hardwood trees are suitable for papermaking. Rainforests are cleared to gain timber for other products and so the land can be used for agriculture. Recycling has many other environmental benefits, though (see page 17).

Forest Resources

Wood is the most important source of energy in any simple society in the world. Many centuries ago, as people began to move around, looking for more land and new opportunities, they had to choose their sites for settlement carefully. Water was the most basic need, but access to a supply of timber was also important so many people settled near woodland or forests.

Fuel

Wood itself has been burned for heating and cooking since prehistoric times. However, the discovery of how to turn wood into charcoal opened up the potential of timber for other uses. From this time, technologies such as smelting metal developed. Charcoal burning is one of the oldest controlled chemical processes in the world. There is evidence of the practice from 4000 BC and the technologies of the Bronze and Iron Ages could not have happened without it. Ancient Egyptians used a substance made from charcoal in the mummifying process. Romans used charcoal in metal production for weapons; they used the waste material from the process in road-building.

An alternative to charcoal was not found until Abraham Darby created coke from coal in the eighteenth century. Coke burned hotter than charcoal and was therefore much more efficient at smelting metals. However, charcoal continued to be put to a number of uses – and it is still used today.

As the Industrial Revolution took hold in the eighteenth and nineteenth centuries, vast swathes of forest were cleared to provide materials for building roads and railways.

CASE STUDY

MEDCs: Sustainable Charcoal Production

Charcoal is still used – for example, in barbecues – in many more economically developed countries (MEDCs). In some regions this has to be imported, and these imports come from the exploitation of valuable rainforest and mangrove swamps. In other countries, however, including the United Kingdom and United States, charcoal is made in the traditional way. This involves coppicing trees (cutting them near the base but leaving them alive to grow further) and then firing the timber in a kiln. Such charcoal industries are sustainable and, if developed further, might stop unsustainable imports.

This charcoal maker in Dorset, UK, is working using traditional methods – the woodland is coppiced, which allows the trees to re-grow.

Transport

Trees have been cut down to use in transport systems for hundreds of years. Ancient peoples used timber to build primitive boats and later, as technologies developed, it was used to build whole fleets of ships.

Wood was used to build roads and railway sleepers, but they would wear out quickly with frequent use, and would have to be replaced regularly. Timber railway sleepers in particular were responsible for huge amounts of deforestation across Europe and North America as the Industrial Revolution gained pace in the nineteenth century, when thousands of kilometres of railways were built and had to be maintained. Timber is still used in railway construction.

Building

Timber was essential for building shelters – either temporary or permanent settlements. Wooden poles were used to hold up tent-like structures used by nomadic peoples such as Native Americans, and logs were used to build sturdier cabins. When European settlers arrived in North America deforestation took off at an incredible rate. About half the land in the region was forested before around 1600 – four million sq km; by 1872 more than half of that had been cleared. As rapid urban development took place more and more forests were cut down to make room and provide the materials needed. It is estimated that a further 93,000 sq km will be cleared by 2050.

Clearance for Farming

People did not only clear forests to use the timber. In many places, the land was needed for farming. In some parts of the world, particularly the Amazonian rainforest, this is still the case. An important method of farming is the 'slash and burn' technique used by people in the Amazon Basin – it is an ancient but completely sustainable way of life. Large trees are cut down using axes ('slash'); small trees are also cut down and their roots are removed. Branches, twigs and other small pieces are gathered together and burned. This burning process clears the land of shrubs and other low-growing vegetation. The ash created by burning the wood is spread evenly over the land; it works as a fertiliser, helping crops to grow in the poor rainforest soil.

Some of the timber that has been cut in this process is used by the rainforest peoples for building homes and as a fuel for cooking. New homes have to be built regularly as the people who live in this way move around from place to place. Firewood is needed every day. Fences are required to keep in animals. The fertility of the soil, even with the added nutrients from the ash, lasts for only two or three years and then the farmers move on to a new piece of land.

The impact of this farming system on the forest is negligible – as long as the population does not become too large the system is sustainable. Each cleared plot of land is allowed to regenerate (revive) naturally. This takes 20 to 30 years, but after that the people can return, clear the forest that has re-grown, and begin the process again.

Fires burn in the Amazon rainforest in Brazil. The 'slash and burn' technique is used to clear land for soya crops.

Then and Now

Although people have cut down areas of woodland and forest to provide for basic heating, building, transport and farming needs for many centuries, it is only relatively recently that such exploitation has become unsustainable. However, the slow but steady clearance of these areas over time has contributed to the situation today, in which the amount of wood available is greatly reduced.

As the world's population continues to grow, more timber will be needed and more trees will be cut down. The consequences of continued deforestation include climate change, lower levels of food production and an increase in the chances of flooding. There is some evidence of this today, but it is not too late to reverse some of the damage and prevent it in the future.

Rainforest peoples build their homes, called *maloccas*, from the timber made available through forest clearance.

CASE STUDY

West and Central Africa: Population Pressures

In West and Central Africa, population growth has put pressure on the 'slash and burn' technique. To feed everyone, either too many plots of land are used too close together, or the fallow (resting) period of 20 to 30 years is shortened to 10 to 15 years. This is not long enough for the nutrients in the soil to return. Heavy rainfall erodes the ground, and the soil and the vegetation are destroyed. Timber can still be cut and individual high-value trees, such as mahogany, can be sold and some money made. However, in the long term, the land and its resources will become unusable.

Timber for furniture

Furniture-making is one of the most widespread uses of timber. On a small scale – where people cut down trees locally to make tables, chairs and other items – this is sustainable. However, the globalisation of trade has made furniture manufacture a thriving industry. Both hardwood and softwood trees are felled on a large scale to feed global demand. The resulting deforestation, as well as the transportation of timber and its products, has had a detrimental effect on the environment.

In full-tree logging, smaller pieces such as branches are turned into chips that can be used for purposes such as fuel, so none of the wood is wasted.

Raw Materials

Cutting trees for any purpose is known as logging or felling. It is an extremely dangerous occupation – loggers work with heavy machinery and heavy logs, as well as dangerous tools such as chainsaws. Such is the demand for wood resources that there are many large plantations employing permanent workforces to cut down the trees to provide timber for furniture. The trees are usually cut close to the base, leaving the stump and the roots in the ground, as digging these out would take too much time and money. There are different cutting methods:

• **Tree-length logging**: after felling, the treetops and branches are removed at the site and only the trunks are transported. The unwanted sections rot, returning nutrients to the soil. This encourages the growth of new trees and although it will take some years, it is a sustainable method of tree-felling.

• **Full-tree logging**: once felled, the whole tree is moved to the nearest road, where the branches are cut away from the log. These are then chipped and the chips are put to a number of uses, including domestic fires, small-scale electricity generation and garden mulch.

Ghana – where these men are making wooden tables for export – has a policy of sustainable forest management. The trees that are cut down are replaced with new stock.

Environmental Impacts of Deforestation

Forests are under tremendous pressure from logging for furniture. Not only are habitats damaged and destroyed, but other economic activities are also damaged. Drinking water is contaminated and greenhouse gases are released.

Removing trees from an ecosystem alters the balance. Biodiversity is reduced and habitats for certain species are lost. Plants that thrive in the shade may die out completely, although others that flourish in sunlight may grow. Trees contain more nutrients than any other parts of an ecosystem, and if these are removed the nutrients that encourage the next generation of plants to grow are dramatically reduced.

FACTS IN FOCUS
The Water Cycle

The water cycle is greatly affected by deforestation. Trees play a large part in slowing down the movement of water through this system. Firstly they catch raindrops, which then drip and flow slowly down to the ground and into the soil. Some water evaporates during this process. Trees then take up water from the soil through their roots and it is returned to the atmosphere. Less rain reaches rivers in a wooded area than in open grassland. Flooding is therefore much less likely.

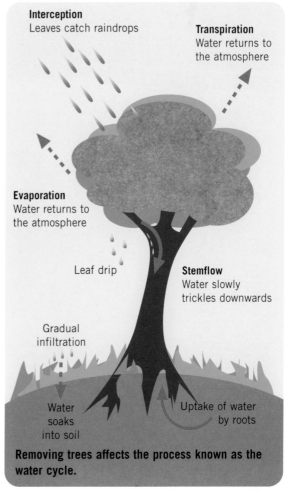

Interception
Leaves catch raindrops

Transpiration
Water returns to the atmosphere

Evaporation
Water returns to the atmosphere

Leaf drip

Stemflow
Water slowly trickles downwards

Gradual infiltration

Water soaks into soil

Uptake of water by roots

Removing trees affects the process known as the water cycle.

Wetland Areas

Cutting down trees near lakes, ponds or wetlands can degrade these precious environments. Machine oil pollutes the water and the heavy equipment used in logging sinks into the damp ground, causing a great deal of damage. Drainage patterns can be affected. Even on dry ground, the weight of the machinery causes the soil to compact and this results in soil erosion, or wearing away. As the soil erodes, landslides can occur more frequently.

Natural Benefits of Logging

It is not all bad news, though. If it is 'low-impact' and managed carefully, logging can have positive effects on the environment. Opening up the canopy by removing a limited number of trees allows light in, encouraging the growth of young trees. Leaving cut branches and treetops on the ground provides habitats for animals and insects – many insects and fungi thrive in decomposing timber. Damaged and diseased trees are removed from the system, which allows healthy trees to grow.

Huge trucks are needed to transport logs from the logging site to processing plants. Noise and air pollution affect the environment.

CASE STUDY

Chile: Timber Exports

Forestry is one of Chile's most rapidly growing economic sectors. The government has recognised the opportunities in growing softwood trees and exporting the timber (instead of native hardwoods). It provides 75 per cent of the money needed for replanting areas of already cut forest with new timber plantations, to encourage farmers to grow more of these trees. This has added 293,000 hectares of extra forest resources. Although this is a positive step, many native forests have been cut down and replaced with plantations, and this has resulted in the loss of some valuable habitats. Environmental groups such as CODEFF and Ancient Forest International have pressured the Chilean government, and now the law states that species of trees that are under threat can no longer be exported. However, their wood can still be used within Chile.

The alerce tree is on the Red List of endangered tree species. It has long been felled in Chile (pictured), but now the law states that these trees can no longer be cut for export.

Transportation

Once cut, most logs are loaded on to large, purpose-built lorries that can transport them great distances. There might be hundreds of kilometres between the site of the logging and the site of the processing plant. Even when the raw timber has been processed, it may have to make another journey to a site where it is manufactured and turned into furniture. Regular flows of timber transport in remote areas cause considerable pressure on the environment, as well as air pollution. Exhaust fumes contribute to acid rain, which in turn damages tree growth, turns their leaves yellow, causing them to drop early in the season. It also reduces their resistance to disease. Rural areas suffer from noise pollution as the trucks rumble through the countryside.

Sometimes the raw material is not manufactured in the country where it originated. Timber or the finished furniture products are exported all over the world, causing further environmental damage. Although in some areas furniture is manufactured on small scales, in local workshops, there are many more companies that manufacture furniture on a huge scale and transport it all over the world.

Timber for Paper

Paper production is essential today, even in a world where more and more communication is electronic and paper-free. Wood is pulped to make books, newspapers, wallpaper, household paper … even money. The paper-manufacturing industry has taken steps to become more sustainable, but there are still a number of ways in which the process could be improved.

Trees for Paper

Many people think that tropical rainforest hardwood trees are cut down to make paper. This is not true – such trees are usually cut for timber for building materials or fuel. Only a few tropical hardwoods can be made into paper, including the black wattle acacia, which grows in Australia and Indonesia. These trees are also grown in eastern and southern Africa for paper production. In North America, hardwood trees such as some types of birch, oak and maple are used to make paper, but increasingly wood from the hardwood eucalyptus is being used all over the world in paper production.

Softwood trees such as pine are ideal for papermaking because they have long fibres that are particularly good for making heavy-duty packaging paper. North America's pines include the loblolly, lodgepole and radiata. South America grows the monkey-puzzle tree (Chile pine) and the radiata pine. In northern Europe the Scots pine mixes with several varieties of spruce. The western hemlock is also an important softwood used for paper.

How Paper is Made

To make paper, wood is ground into fragments, pressed together, dried and bleached with chlorine compounds. There are three main processes, each of which makes a different type of paper.

Chemical Pulping

Chemical pulping is a process that breaks down lignin, the substance that holds the wood together. Once the wood is pulped, it is either bleached to make bright white paper, or it is left unbleached. The unbleached product is used to make bags, boxes and corrugated cardboard. One of the biggest drawbacks of this method is that the chemicals can cause environmental pollution. Some of them are also known to cause cancer.

This chemical processing plant in southern France creates wood pulp from eucalyptus trees.

Paper is stacked awaiting recycling at a paper mill. Recycling paper removes a huge volume of waste from landfill sites, as well as having other environmental benefits (see below).

Mechanical Pulp Processing

Mechanical pulping uses machines to tear apart the wood and to squeeze water out of the pulp. Some chemicals are still used for bleaching, but because fewer chemicals are used in the overall process environmental damage is reduced. However, mechanical pulp processing is less effective; the quality of the paper is not so high, and it turns yellow and disintegrates easily.

Recycling

In the process of recycling the waste is first collected, sorted, baled and then transported from recycling sites to paper-recycling mills. There it is re-pulped to turn it back into individual fibres. Chemicals are added to separate out inks, coatings and other additives from the original paper. The contaminants float to the surface as a scum, which is skimmed off and the pulp is then treated like pulp straight from wood. A major environmental issue with recycling is disposing of the scum waste. Recycled paper is often bleached and chlorine chemicals can get into rivers near the processing plants. Transporting the paper from the recycling sites to the mills is expensive and causes pollution.

Although recycling is less polluting than other methods, it is still not perfect. In fact, papermaking is one of the most environmentally damaging industries in the world.

FACTS IN FOCUS

Recycling –
The Environmental Savings

Supermarket shelves stock many recycled paper products, including tissues, kitchen paper and toilet paper. They may not look as white and clean as paper processed in other ways, but does that really matter? For every tonne of paper used for recycling, the savings over non-recycled products are:

- At least 30,000 litres of water
- 3,000–4,000 KwH electricity (enough for a three-bedroom house for a year)
- 95 per cent of the air pollution

CASE STUDY

United States: Fox River

Fox River runs into Lake Michigan in the United States. It is one of the most polluted rivers in the country due to chemicals released from seven large paper mills in the area. Most of the pollution comes from PCBs (polychlorinated biphenyls), which are chemicals used in ink. PCBs can be absorbed through the skin by people swimming or fishing in Lake Michigan. They are also absorbed by the wildlife such as fish and ducks. There are currently no effective alternatives for the use of PCBs in papermaking, so different methods of disposal must be found.

Locals in the Fox River area and environmental groups have campaigned for a clean-up operation and for regulations that will control the policies of the paper mills, although the companies have not broken any laws. In November 2007 the companies were ordered to begin a process of dredging the contaminated sediment from the river and disposing of it in a landfill site.

The Qingai River in the Sichuan Province of China is heavily polluted by the activities of a nearby paper mill, releasing toxic waste into the water.

Tree Farms

Once cut for paper, forests are often replaced with tree farms. In most cases these farms are made up of a single species of tree, and this means a much poorer habitat for wildlife. Biodiversity (the variety of plants, insects and animals that live in a particular area) is dramatically reduced. One severe case is in Sweden. The large-scale felling of trees for papermaking here has resulted in the loss of many species. Trees cannot grow again on the land because the soil has eroded. The Swedish Society for Nature Conservation publicised this practice in an attempt to stop it. It is also one of the many organisations that has signed the Vision for Transforming the European Paper Industry, a campaign to reduce paper use and encourage more sustainable methods of paper production.

Air Pollution

In mechanical pulp mills levels of air pollution are fairly low, and are caused mainly by the fuel being burned. However, chemical pulp mills send out more damaging gases, including hydrogen sulphide and oxides of sulphur and nitrogen. Recycling paper actually causes higher levels of air pollution than other methods because the sludge that is skimmed off from ink and other chemicals from the first use of the paper has to be incinerated. The burning process is responsible for the air pollution.

Toxic Waste

The bleaching process creates environmental pollutants such as dioxin, which can cause cancer, and mercury, which is poisonous to plants, animals and people. All forms of papermaking can result in these chemicals being released into local waterways. Research is underway to develop a process called biological pulping. This is similar to chemical pulping but it uses species of fungi to break down the fibres instead of chemicals. This would greatly reduce the amount of pollution created by current methods.

Intensive Energy Use

Processing paper from wood needs huge amounts of energy, and this also has an environmental

impact. In 2007, for example, the pulp and paper industry in the United States contributed nine per cent of the nation's manufacturing industry carbon emissions.

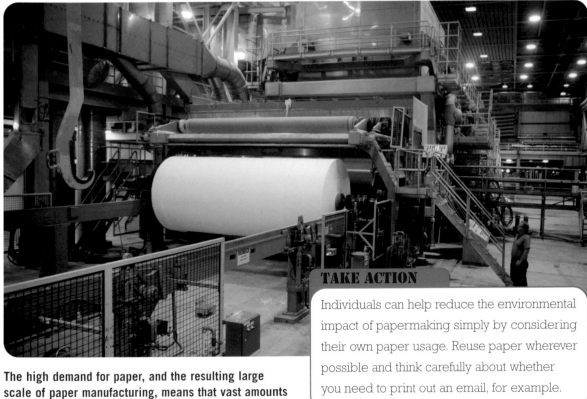

The high demand for paper, and the resulting large scale of paper manufacturing, means that vast amounts of energy are consumed in the process.

Water Consumption

Paper manufacturing requires large amounts of water, and paper mills are often situated alongside rivers (such as Fox River, see page 18). Chemical pulping uses between 159,000 and 204,000 litres of water for every tonne of paper produced. Mechanical pulping is less devastating, at only 45,000 to 68,000 litres per tonne. The water is channelled from the river and used in the processing. It is then returned to its source. The temperature of the water can rise as a result of this use. The use of underground water sources can cause a drop in the water table.

Transporting Paper

From the beginning of the papermaking process many road miles are driven: timber to pulp mill; pulp to paper mill; paper to printer or other manufacturer; finished product to warehouse or shop. All this transportation contributes to air pollution and the use of valuable fossil fuels. One way of addressing the transport problem in this and other areas of timber use is to have the buildings for various stages of the process closer to one another, and to encourage the local manufacture of paper products.

Landfill

A great deal of paper ends up in landfill sites because people do not make the effort to recycle it. Solid chemical waste from paper manufacture also has to be disposed of. The heightened awareness of the problems of landfill has resulted in some positive steps, however. Increasingly,

Giant rolls of paper are loaded on to a lorry ready for transportation from the manufacturer.

CASE STUDY

India: Tamil Nadu Paper Mill

The Tamil Nadu paper mill in India is the largest in the world to use wood-free processes. Instead, the paper is made from sugar-cane fibres, known as *bagasse*. Because it is not a wood product no forests are felled to acquire the raw material. The sugar cane does not even have to be grown specially for paper-making because *bagasse* is a waste product from the sugar-refining industry. The paper still needs to be bleached and chemicals are used for this process, but the environmental impact is far less damaging than traditional papermaking methods. Other countries are now beginning to follow India's lead and using wood-free processes.

A worker on a hemp farm measures the crop, which is being grown for wood-free papermaking.

companies are incinerating (burning) a lot of their paper waste, which is much more environmentally friendly than leaving it for landfill.

Non-wood Fibre for Papermaking

Fibres for paper manufacture do not need to come from wood – other plants can provide them, and their environmental impact is far smaller than wood-based papermaking. Hemp, flax and kenaf are all grown for paper. Wetland plants grow quickly, so papyrus, rushes and water hyacinth can also be used. Waste from food crops, like straw from cereals, can also be used.

Environmental impacts depend on the method of production of these crops. Organic crops are ideal, as no chemicals are involved. If part of a crop-rotation system, soil will be conserved. These waste fibres would otherwise go to landfill or incineration, so turning them into paper is a better end product. Pulping agricultural fibres can cause pollution, as chemicals are used, but the amount of damage per tonne of paper is significantly lower than other methods.

EXPERT VIEW

'Most of the studies support the view that recycling and incineration are environmentally preferable to landfill. There is less agreement on whether recycling is preferable to incineration. Critical factors are the nature of the pulp and papermaking process, the level of technology at all stages of the life cycle and the energy structure of the countries under study.'
'TOWARDS A SUSTAINABLE PAPER CYCLE', A STUDY BY THE INTERNATIONAL INSTITUTE FOR ENVIRONMENT AND DEVELOPMENT

Timber for Building

Timber-frame houses have been used for centuries, in both traditional and modern societies. Many buildings more than 250 years old are still standing and are in regular use. Timber might seem like an old-fashioned material for building projects, but its value has been proved, and in many cases it remains preferable to some more modern materials. While the demand for timber for building has depleted tree stocks, there are several environmental benefits to its use.

Timber-frame construction is more popular than ever today. In the United Kingdom 78 per cent of new homes are built in this way; in North America and Scandinavia that figure is as high as 95 per cent. The timber frame is covered on the outside by bricks and on the inside by plasterboard, so the finished house does not look any different from one made with breeze blocks (concrete). However, a timber-framed house takes less time to build because workers do not need to allow time for wet mortar to dry out. Timber is also light but very strong and durable.

Advantages of Using Wood

Timber-frame houses can be divided up inside in many different ways. A number of small rooms can be created, or a large space can be left for an open-plan living area. It takes less time to build using a timber frame than it does using other materials – only two to three days for the frame itself. Computer-guided tools cut the pieces of timber to the right size and shape in a factory before they are transported to the building site. Even the fitting together of pieces can be tested in the factory and holes drilled in the right places, making a basic construction kit.

Using timber frames for houses and other buildings is a popular construction method.

Keeping a house warm is important as energy costs rise and the need to conserve energy increases. Insulating a timber-frame house is easy: the spaces are there – they just need to be filled with a suitable material. One of the most recent ideas is the use of sheep's wool as insulation. Timber itself can also insulate, in the form of recycled newspaper. This is a simple idea and inexpensive to carry out. These natural materials keep a house cool in summer and warm in winter. There is no risk of skin irritation or breathing in dangerous fibres, which fibreglass insulation can cause.

Disadvantages of Using Wood

Timber buildings can be noisier than other structures; footsteps can be heard in neighbouring rooms. Because it is a natural material, wood can suffer from infestations of insects like termites, cockroaches or powderpost beetles. Vermin such as mice, rats and bats are happy to make their homes there too. Wood can rot in both wet and dry conditions, but the timber used today is usually treated to protect against infestations or decay. Wood burns more readily than most other materials, so more severe damage is likely in a fire.

Because wood is a natural material it can suffer from infestations by termites.

Parquet flooring is popular in houses, and can provide good insulation.

Flooring, Staircases and Window Frames

Timber is not just used for building frames. It is put to use in other ways too. Many houses have parquet floors – long, thin strips of wood that fit together to make symmetrical patterns. Making and laying parquet flooring is a labour-intensive task, so the finished product is expensive. Laminate flooring is also popular. Some laminate is made of man-made materials and just created to look like wood, but the best is made of real wood, with tongue-and-groove edges that fit together perfectly. This provides good insulation. Chipboard flooring is made from waste wood so it is low-cost and its production has a less damaging effect on the environment.

Stairs are usually made of wood. Flexible and easy to shape, wood looks attractive, fits into a limited space, and can be shaped and curved as necessary. Different woods give a range of colours and effects. Window frames are also traditionally made of wood. If seasoned (treated to last), these will remain in good condition for decades. However, many modern houses use unseasoned timber, which needs replacing every few years.

Alternative Materials

Timber is used for building in all these different ways because it is so adaptable, and recent developments have made it even more so. Structured Insulated Panel (SIP) technology is a method in which insulation is built into wall and floor panels in the factory.

Timber is less suitable for larger buildings like office blocks. Steel, concrete and glass are more appropriate materials for these types of building.

These houses in Manchester, UK, are part of a scheme to create environmentally friendly homes. They have Structured Insulated Panel (SIP) roofs.

Steel can be recycled, so it is more environmentally friendly than other materials, but making steel uses a great deal of energy – five or six times as much as producing timber for building purposes.

Newer developments include polystyrene houses. These have no frame of timber or steel, which helps them resist earthquake shaking in all three dimensions. Polystyrene houses may prove valuable in countries at risk from earthquakes like Pakistan and Iran.

Garden Structures

Sheds are common in gardens and on allotments. Most come as kits, with all the wooden pieces ready to assemble. Despite changes in fashion, the main material used to manufacture garden furniture is still timber. Hardwoods are more popular than softwoods because they are more resistant to weather. Teak, an important rainforest species, is the most popular. Both sustainable and non-sustainable timber is available; as consumers become more aware of the environmental issues surrounding deforestation, many are choosing wood that has been grown sustainably.

Coastal Defences

Groynes and revetments are both structures used to defend coastlines against sea erosion. They look like fences, built at right angles to the shore. They are usually made of tropical hardwoods because these cope better with regular wetting and drying from the waves. Groynes have a life of 15 to 20 years, after which they must be replaced.

FACTS IN FOCUS
Permafrost

Lightweight wooden buildings are often used in Arctic regions. They have double walls with efficient insulation in the space, so they are warm. Windows are triple glazed. Permafrost zones – areas where the ground is frozen most of the year – need special adaptations to their wooden buildings, but wood itself is not the best material for all purposes. The ground surface thaws during the short summer, so normal foundations would come under pressure and crack. To avoid this, the wooden structure is supported on concrete or steel stilts going deep into the solid permafrost, which is unaffected by surface melting.

Revetments, a cheaper alternative to sea walls, can also be timber. They cost about £1,200 per metre, whereas sea walls can be as much as £5,000. Wooden posts are driven into the beach, often with metal to protect them. Fixed between them is a lattice of sloping, slatted planks that break the energy of the wave when it hits. Water, sand and pebbles pass through the gaps. Placed along the base of a cliff, they protect it from erosion.

Groynes must be replaced every 15 or 20 years. This uses more wood, but the environmental impact of coastal erosion is reduced.

FACTS IN FOCUS
Green Waste

Some wood waste can be made into peat-free compost. This can be a long process – between 12 and 20 weeks – because the waste must be sterilised. However, this compost can be used on farms and in gardens, and is a good way to put wood waste to another use. Sources of green waste include local household waste recycling centres, nurseries, tree surgeons and landscape-gardening firms.

Do We Use Too Much Wood?

Timber is the most sustainable building material available. It is organic, non-toxic and completely renewable. In Europe and North America softwoods are largely used for construction and these are produced sustainably. Ninety-nine per cent of all building timber used in Europe is softwood grown within the continent, which reduces the environmental impact of global transportation (although it must sometimes still travel long distances). More trees are planted than are harvested in North America and Europe, so forest area is increasing. Tropical deforestation is not caused by house building in MEDCs.

Due to careful forest management, European countries such as Germany are now experiencing a rise in forest areas rather than a decline.

Wood production is almost carbon neutral, meaning that it generates less carbon dioxide than other materials and products, and therefore contributes less to global warming. In addition, at the end of its useful life in a building, wood can be recycled into something else, extending its usefulness. It takes a great deal of effort to demolish concrete buildings, and even when they have been destroyed, the waste material ends up in landfill sites, where it does not decompose in the way that wood does. Wood is one of the best materials for building – as long as the trees from which the timber is acquired are grown in a sustainable way.

Sustainable Building Programmes

Since there is no more sustainable material than timber, as new communities become 'greener' – more aware of the changes needed to slow down or prevent environmental damage – demand for more sustainable living will increase. The largest housing development zone in the United Kingdom in the early twenty-first century was the Thames Gateway, east of London. This was planned as a completely sustainable community, where houses, energy supply and transport systems are all environmentally friendly. Timber frames for houses are ideal where energy-saving systems are installed, because wood is effective at keeping warmth in.

CASE STUDY

Sweden: Hammarby Sjöstad

Hammarby Sjöstad is a sustainable housing development in Stockholm, Sweden, built on a former industrial site on the shores of a lake. It is intended to house 20,000 people, with another 10,000 coming in to work each day. The site will have houses of all different sizes and designs. All the buildings will be made of natural, recyclable materials, using less energy and water. The district will have a sustainable transport network. Hammarby's power will be supplied by incinerated waste, which will provide hot water for central heating and steam for electricity generation. Roofs will be 'green' – they will catch rainwater and slow its movement into the drains to prevent flooding. The project is scheduled for completion in 2016.

Hammarby Sjöstad is designed to be completely sustainable in terms of building materials, energy supply and transport systems.

Timber for fuel

Fuel wood is the most important form of energy in LEDCs. In terms of global warming it is a completely sustainable fossil fuel, since the amount of carbon dioxide given off during burning is no more than that absorbed by the tree or shrub as it grew. In terms of resources, however, timber that is cut down must be replaced and given enough time to re-grow fully.

In Nepal, high mountain regions of forest were once cleared. Although some areas still show signs of deforestation, the situation is improving and forest cover is increasing. It is a different story in lowland areas.

Fuel wood is essential in rural Africa, Asia and South America for cooking and warmth. It is free, collected from the natural environment by the user. Population growth places great pressure on this resource. As supplies reduce, people have to walk further to collect enough wood for their needs. It can become a task that takes all day, just to be able to cook the family evening meal. Often people are poor – they cannot buy other fuel resources and do not have the money to buy new plants to replace those taken. Desertification is a consequence of this pressure placed on the vegetation.

Disaster in Nepal

Between 1965 and 1980, lowland regions of Nepal lost around 20 per cent of their forest cover. This was largely to pay the high taxes demanded by the government. Since the 1990s the situation has worsened, with 200 hectares of forest being destroyed daily. A trade dispute with India had cut off Nepal's oil imports and timber replaced oil as a fuel for most Nepalese. Government corruption meant logging permits were illegally issued to foreign companies and timber was sold at one-third of its true value.

This had a serious effect on the country's economy and on the lives of the local people.

The results of this deforestation affect not only the Nepali people, but also those who live lower down the Ganges River basin, some of whose tributaries flow from Nepal. Deforestation leads to soil erosion, the silting up of rivers and potentially disastrous flooding. This has been seen especially in Bangladesh.

CASE STUDY

Kenya: Korr

About 3.5 million people in north-east Kenya have lost their livelihoods as the Sahara Desert spreads southwards. Korr is a recent settlement in this region; it has grown rapidly because it has a water source, which is rare in desert regions. Deep wells can be dug here to provide for nomadic people and their livestock. Many people have even given up their nomadic way of life and settled here; shops and services are now provided – but all this places pressure on a limited water resource. The concentration of animals has removed the grazing; the concentration of people has removed the fuel wood. Pressure on resources is huge in this environmentally fragile area.

Korr has hope, however. Aid projects have helped. Land has been fenced off and planted with grass and trees. Animals are only allowed to graze in certain areas. High-yielding fuel-wood species have been planted. Drought-resistant, high-yielding dairy goats have been bred. All these factors are contributing to a more sustainable future for Korr.

In the dry desert landscape of Korr, people rely on a precious water source for survival. However, the influx of settlers to the area has put pressure on other resources such as wood.

What is Desertification?

Desertification occurs when a desert spreads into a neighbouring area of semi-desert. Natural changes to climate can cause this, but human activity is also a big contributor to desertification. Land is often used too intensively. Too many animals graze, too many trees and shrubs are cut, too much water is taken from the ground. Extensive desertification has been taking place in Africa, as the Sahara Desert spreads southwards into the Sahel region. It is also happening in southern Africa and India. In the mid-twentieth century a period of wetter weather in the Sahel resulted in a slowing of desertification. This meant that more animals could graze on the land, and this in turn supported the people who lived there. However, in the 1970s the climate became drier again and drought hit the region. Both animals and people died. What can be done to prevent this kind of desertification?

Resisting Drought

One solution is to plant species of trees and shrubs that can survive in even the driest conditions. The best method of collecting fuel is coppicing. This technique was used in early medieval Europe, and involves cutting a tree near its base without killing it. The tree grows again, sending up shoots that become slim trunks. These can be harvested in the future, over a much longer period, and each tree is more productive in its lifetime.

Wood Pellets as Fuel

Wood pellets, made from compacted sawdust – waste material from sawmills – make an extremely efficient fuel because they are very dense and contain less than 10 per cent moisture. Wood pellets can be used in wood burners that run central heating systems and water heaters. Available since 1999, they are becoming

BELOW: The Sahel region of Africa is one of the worst-hit by desertification – the encroachment of desert into semi-desert areas. Precious resources such as trees die out and people can no longer live there.

increasingly popular and, as fossil fuels dramatically increase in price, sales may improve further. Wood pellets are a convenient fuel because:

- They are very dense (they do not even float in water). They can be stored and transported efficiently because fewer are needed to provide the same burning capacity as other fuels.
- Any wood can be used
- They are a recycled product in that they would otherwise be wasted
- No carbon dioxide is produced in the process, since the amount given off in the burning is the same as that absorbed by the tree in growth

Austria has more pellet central-heating systems per person than anywhere in the world, and two-thirds of all new systems use this method. Italy, Germany and Scandinavia are not far behind.

Wood pellets are a useful and sustainable form of fuel, and one that is increasingly being used in parts of Europe.

EXPERT VIEW

'Desertification is a worldwide problem that poses a severe challenge to the more than 1.2 billion people in more than 100 countries… Desertification does not so much refer to the spread of existing deserts as the creation of new ones, through the reduction of productivity of dry land areas by soil deterioration and erosion as well as the long-term loss of natural vegetation.'
MADRID CONFERENCE OF THE UNITED NATIONS CONVENTION TO COMBAT DESERTIFICATION, 2007

Rainforest Logging

On both local and national levels, the destruction of large areas of rainforest has had a dramatic effect on biodiversity. Habitats are lost so that plants, insects and animals can no longer survive. They cannot adapt quickly to the sudden, dramatic change in their environment. Once key plants are gone, food sources for insects and animals are lost. The area is altered, if not forever, then certainly for many lifetimes.

Deforestation dramatically changes the amount of water in soil, rock and in the atmosphere, and the water cycle is severely affected. Instead of trapping rain in the tree canopy and letting it trickle slowly to the soil and into the ground, a bare landscape does not absorb water. Most rain flows as surface water, which causes soil erosion. The new farmland created by rainforest clearance can actually only be used for a short time before it becomes worthless, so the benefits are short-term.

In this part of Brazil, south of Maranhao State, rainforest logging is illegal, but continues to be a booming trade.

Trees also cycle large amounts of water back to the air, so when they are cut down rainfall is reduced – often over a large area. North and north-west China is severely deforested, and the amount of rainfall decreased by a third between 1950 and 1980. There are often dramatic news stories about climate change and global warming – and deforestation is partly responsible for this.

Why is Rainforest Cleared?

In the past, using the rainforest for agriculture put little pressure on the ecosystem – it was sustainable. Today, however, the large scale of its destruction is unsustainable. There are several reasons for rainforest clearance.

Demand for Food

Huge tracts of Amazonia have been deforested to provide land for grazing beef cattle to supply the growing number of fast-food outlets across the world. The increasing wealth of many developing countries, especially in Asia, means the size of this market is expanding.

Farming

Soya is the latest foodstuff to be produced large scale on cleared rainforest land. Most is used for vegetable

Drilling for oil beneath the rainforest requires the felling of trees and attracts people to the area, further depleting resources.

oil and animal feed. Farmers often take over public land illegally, deforesting it using cheap labour. They are funded by multinational companies, which buy the harvested crop. Environmental pressure groups like Greenpeace have publicised this illegal soya issue and some improvements have been seen.

Logging for Timber

Demand for furniture hardwood was the earliest cause of significant rainforest loss. Because these trees grow individually rather than in groups, many other trees are destroyed in the process of obtaining the mahogany, teak or rosewood chosen. Today, the most active logging companies operate in Southeast Asia.

Mining

The Amazon Basin contains huge mineral wealth, but the forest is in the way. Wide road access is also needed for trucks to remove the mined ores. The trucks damage the soil and cause erosion. Gold needs mercury – a poison – for extraction, leading to huge damage to surrounding forest and wildlife.

Oil Drilling

Oil companies are actively searching for resources beneath rainforest. Roads and pipelines are being built through untouched forest. Settlers are encouraged by these roads, and slash and burn and charcoal production begin.

Dam Building

The World Bank gives loans to build dams in LEDCs for electricity generation. Vast areas of rainforest are flooded.

Economic Impacts of Logging in Indonesia

Indonesia's large logging industry exploits timber primarily for furniture. Loss of rainforest plants and animals is especially significant because this country has the largest number of mammal species in the world, 17 per cent of all the world's birds and 20,000 plant species (as well as others that have not even been identified). Many species are facing extinction because of the logging.

The people who live in the rainforest are suffering because of the actions of large companies, many of which are backed by the government. There have been lengthy battles between the Moi people and the Intimpura Timber Company, which is threatening their way of life. The government granted logging licences that allowed the company to clearfell forest, despite the fact that the Moi used it for farming.

The pollution of land, air and water has also caused economic problems in the region. Soil erosion has caused silting of rivers and flooding. Oil spills from machinery pollute soil and water.

Air Pollution in Southeast Asia

In Southeast Asia fires are started as part of a technique to clear the rainforests. The worst fires occurred in 1997–98, when they started to burn out of control, but this method is still being used for forest clearance. The fires cause serious air pollution. Fires in Borneo and Indonesia blanketed Malaysia and Singapore with thick smoke. The elderly and sick were told to remain indoors. Satellite photos revealed the huge area affected across Southeast Asia. The situation was worsened by the cities' own industrial and traffic pollutants being trapped beneath the sinking smoke.

In Indonesia 20 million people were affected by throat or respiratory infections or diarrhoea. In Malaysia, sprinklers were mounted on some of the tallest buildings to wash some of the pollutants out of the air, but the thick haze continued, closing schools, offices and public buildings.

OPPOSITE: This satellite image shows smoke rising from nearly 1,000 forest fires burning in Indonesia in 2003.

Policemen in Indonesia raid a lorry filled with illegally logged timber.

FACTS IN FOCUS

Forest losses in Ethiopia and Indonesia

Ethiopia lost 98 per cent of its forests between 1955 and 2005. Thirty-five per cent of this country used to be covered with forests, around 420,000 sq km.

Estimated rainforest losses in Indonesia are:

1970s	300,000 ha/year
1980s	600,000 ha/year
1990s	1 million ha/year

Looking to the future

In 2007, 300 scientists attended the Bali Climate Conference in Indonesia. They agreed that if too much forest is cut, the battle against global warming will be lost. The amount of carbon dioxide that burning forests puts into the atmosphere is far greater than the amount caused by transport. If all the rainforest was destroyed, atmospheric carbon dioxide concentration would increase by 25 per cent. Keeping forests as a carbon store is very important.

Global Warming

Carbon is one of the most important elements for growing plants. The carbon mixes with oxygen from the air to form carbon dioxide. Green plants take this in through their leaves in the process of photosynthesis; it is then turned into glucose, which the plant needs to grow. Some of the carbon is stored in the plant, but burning releases this into the atmosphere, where it becomes carbon dioxide again, increasing the temperature of the Earth's atmosphere.

If global warming worsens, the forests themselves will suffer. In North America a 2°C temperature rise will destroy the ideal habitat for many forest species. They would have to move about 300 km north to find the ideal climate. Most species could not move this distance. Higher temperatures would also mean drier conditions and more forest fires.

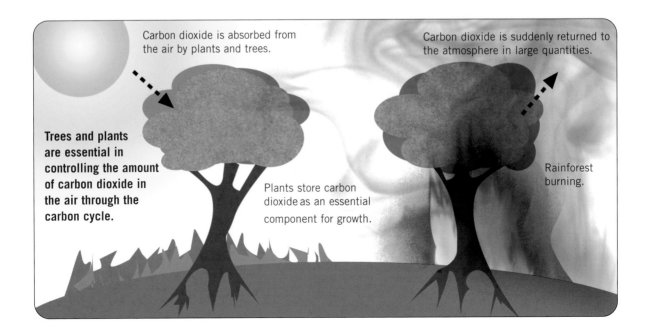

Carbon dioxide is absorbed from the air by plants and trees.

Carbon dioxide is suddenly returned to the atmosphere in large quantities.

Trees and plants are essential in controlling the amount of carbon dioxide in the air through the carbon cycle.

Plants store carbon dioxide as an essential component for growth.

Rainforest burning.

Acacia trees flourish on the edge of the Sahel, demonstrating the success of re-afforestation.

The 'tipping point' – the moment when the long-term effects of climate change can no longer be prevented – is 2018. This deadline has made governments all over the world consider how best to address the problem. At the Bali conference, negotiations started about compensating poorer countries for keeping their forest reserves in the future.

Afforestation

Afforestation means planting trees in areas where there were none. It is not always easy because conditions may not be suitable for trees to flourish. Soil might be thin and poor quality, so planting new deciduous trees is impractical. In the 1970s several European countries began establishing coniferous plantations. These caused a lot of debate. Some people argued that the dark green conifers were gloomy to look at, others that the straight lines of tree planting were unnatural. Others, however, argued that some trees were better than no trees. They also improved the economies of these areas, as the trees could be cut, one section at a time, for pulp and paper and then sustainably replaced. Over time people have become used to the different landscape.

Re-afforestation

Regions devastated by deforestation can be reclaimed with care. Satellite images taken in 1986 and 2006 show that areas of desert are shrinking as new acacia trees are planted. Once they become established, shade and water are more plentiful so agriculture can begin again, improving standards of living for thousands of extremely poor people. Three million hectares of Niger have been replanted, after too much fuel wood was harvested and the land being poorly managed had devastated the area. A quarter of a million hectares of new food crops are now growing, supported by the richer ecosystem encouraged by the woodland.

EXPERT VIEW

'For once there is some good news from Africa. Farmers are reclaiming the desert, turning the barren wastelands of the Sahel region on the Sahara's southern edge into green, productive farmland.'
ANDY COGHLAN, NEW SCIENTIST, 14 OCTOBER 2006

The United States has some of the largest tree nurseries in the world, some of which produce over 100 million seedlings every year.

Difficulties of Re-afforestation

The most difficult environment for re-afforestation is rainforest because the soil has so few nutrients in it, which makes it difficult for new trees to thrive. Also, soils erode very quickly after deforestation, so sometimes there is not enough soil for new trees to take root. Tree nurseries have been set up to nurture seedlings ready to replant in the wild. Several tropical countries now run such projects, including Malawi, Botswana, Burundi, Ethiopia, Kenya, Lesotho, South Africa, Madagascar, Rwanda, Somalia, Tanzania and Sri Lanka. Their aim is to improve damaged rainforest. More developed countries, like the United States, United Kingdom and New Zealand, use tree nurseries to produce seedlings for plantations for pulp, paper and building timber.

Agroforestry

Agroforestry means production of forest species that are also crops (called 'cash crops'). Cocoa, for example, comes from the cacao tree, a West African rainforest species, which is now grown in areas outside Africa, including Indonesia. Income is greater if the canopy is cleared so the tree crops get maximum sunlight, but this system is unsustainable.

In the longer term, income is steadier if the canopy is thinned, allowing sun to get to the cacao trees while still protecting the ground and maintaining a flourishing ecosystem. Research has shown that if canopy cover (normally 80 per cent) is reduced to 40 per cent, yields and therefore income are doubled, without any negative effect on the environment.

Other cash crops are grown in MEDCs. Walnuts are grown throughout the central Valley of California and in the Coast Range valleys between Redding and Bakersfield, in the United States. Trees are carefully tended, sprayed, irrigated and fertilised. Pruning is done by hand but picking can be mechanised. A mechanical shaker makes the nuts fall; then they are air-blown together so the mechanical harvester can pick them up.

More and more programmes to establish sustainable tree crops are being set up to improve income and environment in areas where people struggle to use damaged land. The STCP – Sustainable Tree Crops Programme – is developing sustainable cocoa, coffee and cashew tree crop systems in Africa. Farmers' organisations, governments, international development agencies, academic researchers and even some food-industry representatives helped to plan this programme.

OPPOSITE: Cocoa beans are dried in the sun. Cacao plantations in West Africa offer a sustainable agroforestry solution to economic problems.

FACTS IN FOCUS
Malawi Tree Nursery

Already a very poor country, Malawi loses precious resources daily. An area of rainforest the size of a football pitch is lost every 10 minutes. Overpopulation is the cause – more land is needed for agriculture. The Earth Restoration Service Tree Nursery Programme in Malawi aims to grow four million trees every year. Four hundred community nurseries would each grow 10,000 trees a year. Local communities would be managing their own environment sustainably and poverty would reduce. The aims are:

- To preserve the existing tree cover
- To replace much of what has been felled in the Nkhata Bay District of Malawi

Trees for Shading Other Crops

Another sustainable method of agriculture is using trees to shade other crops. This works particularly well in coffee production. Most coffee is 'sun-grown', in the open, on plantations. Forest must be cleared to make way for these plantations. Recently, an alternative of 'shade grown' has become popular. Coffee is a shrub and can be grown beneath full-sized rainforest trees so they do not need to be felled. In these areas the quality of the soil is not damaged, so there is no need for chemical fertilisers. Forest litter acts as mulch.

The forest structure of a shade coffee farm provides a perfect habitat for hundreds of species of birds, insects (especially butterflies), bats, reptiles and mammals. More sun-grown coffee can be grown per hectare, but the environmental benefits of the alternative are huge.

Forests in the Future

If traditional rainforest farming methods are built into present-day agricultural projects, the results are more likely to be sustainable. Systems like agroforestry avoid rainforest destruction and provide income for poor farmers. Patches of mixed crop fields and pasture within the rainforest can increase production and reduce forest destruction.

If sustainable agriculture systems like this are to survive and expand they must be profitable. People will not use these methods if they cannot make a good living. Transport of goods to market is very important. Roads must be built, even though this involves some rainforest destruction. Farmers must also be able to borrow money at low rates of interest; otherwise they cannot set up a profitable rainforest farm.

CASE STUDY

South America: Rainforest Concern

Rainforests in Ecuador, South America, are between 60 and 150 million years old and are still evolving. Estimates suggest 30 million species of animals, plants, insects and fungi live in rainforests worldwide – half of all living species. Rainforest Concern is a charity working in Ecuador to conserve and protect these species. One of their projects, the Choco-Andean Rainforest Corridor, has been classified as a World Biodiversity Hotspot, because of its huge variety of species. Some areas, such as the Awa Bioreserve and parts of the cloud forest, are already protected. The idea of the 'corridor' is to link together the three largest protected parts of Ecuador. Biological corridors allow animal and plant migration, creating healthy population levels.

The cloud forest of the Awa Bioreserve in Colombia.

This farmer in Brazil is adding an organic fertiliser to his shade-grown coffee.

TAKE ACTION

Try to buy shade-grown coffee – the packaging clearly states how it has been grown.

Today there are 600 million poor tropical farmers and the number increases by five per cent every year as population grows. These people need the right opportunities to be able to exploit forests and semi-wooded areas effectively.

Charity Campaigns

Of the many charities involved in rainforest conservation projects, the WWF is probably the best known. This buys areas for conservation, encourages responsible forestry, maintains clean lakes, works with local conservation groups and global organisations. DfID (UK Department for International Development), USAID (United States Agency for International Development),

the European Union, the World Bank and HSBC (Hong Kong and Shanghai Banking Corporation) are global examples, and Imazon (Amazon Institute of People and the Environment) is a local conservation group in the rainforest.

Seventeen per cent of the Amazon forest had been lost by 2007 so it is a case of getting everyone to support, whether on a large or small scale. Looking to the future, between 2007 and 2030, Amazon deforestation alone could release between 55.5 and 96.9 billion tonnes of carbon dioxide into the atmosphere. If large-scale action is not taken by individuals, charities, companies and global organisations, an important stabiliser of the world's climate will be destroyed.

facts and figures

Annual Deforestation in the Amazon

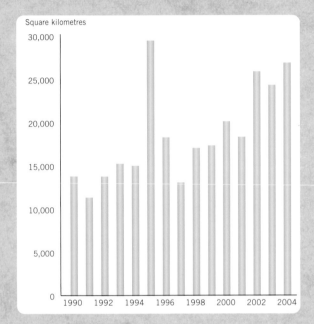

Square kilometres

Timber from Plantations: How Much Land Would We Need?

We use 3.5 billion cubic metres per year and 350 million hectares (1 hectare = a square whose sides are each 100 m long) should provide this. This is 2.7 per cent of the Earth's land surface. However, in the future, demand will probably double, so 5.5 per cent of land will need to be used for sustainable plantations. With huge effort and co-operation from everyone concerned, this is possible – but it is nevertheless a huge challenge.

Forest Areas by Country

Country	% Land Area that is Forest
Afghanistan	1.3
Angola	47.4
Argentina	12.1
Australia	21.3
Bangadesh	6.7
Bhutan	68.0
Brazil	56.5
Canada	34.1
Chad	9.5
China	21.2
Costa Rica	46.8
Democratic Republic of Congo	58.9
France	28.3
Germany	31.7
India	22.8
Indonesia	48.8
Israel	7.9
Japan	68.2
Madagascar	22.1
Malaysia	63.6
Mexico	33.7
Nepal	25.4
Nigeria	12.2
Norway	30.7
Peru	53.7
Saudi Arabia	1.3
South Africa	7.6
Spain	35.9
Sweden	67.1
Thailand	28.4
United Kingdom	11.8
United States	33.1
Venezuela	54.1

further Resources

Websites

Timber for Building

http://www.today.plus.com/houses/page2.html
Early timber homes.

www.usaid.gov/stories/pakistan/ss_pk_artisans.html
Problem buildings in Pakistan earthquake.

www.timber-frame.org
Timber-frame buildings.

http://www.hockertonhousingproject.org.uk
A sustainable timber building project.

http://www.loghomes.com
Modern log cabins in North America.

Timber for Paper

http://www.paper.org.uk/info/treesused.htm
Trees used in the paper industry.

http://www.42explore.com/papermaking.htm
The papermaking process.

Other Wood Uses

http://www.users.globalnet.co.uk/~drayner/coastman.htm
Various coastal defence strategies.

http://www.ypte.org.uk/docs/factsheets/env_facts/
rainffmedfood.html
Medicines from the rainforest.

Tree Crops

http://www.walnutinfo.com
Walnut production.

http://rainforest-alliance.org
Coffee production and other crops.

http://www.shadecoffee.org
Shade coffee production.

http://www.cocoafederation.com
Cocoa production.

Forest Exploitation

http://www.forestry.gov.uk
Forestry Commission Great Britain.

www.American.edu/ted/chile.htm
Timber exploitation in Chile.

http://www.illegal-logging.info
Illegal deforestation.

Forest Protection and Sustainability

http://www.globaltrees.org
Global Trees Campaign.

http://www.greenpeace.org.uk
Many types of global conservation.

http://www.panda.org
World Wide Fund for Nature.

http://www.adoption.co.uk/rainforest/
Rainforest Concern charity.

http://www.veeriku.tartu.ee/~ppensa/Acacia1.jpg
Acacia planting to improve ecosystems.

http://www.earthrestorationservice.org/page/106/malawi
-tree-nursery.htm
Tree nurseries in Malawi.

Books

Champion, Neil, *Tropical Rainforests* (Caring for the Planet), Smart Apple Media, 2006

Dubois, Philippe J. and Valerie Guidoux, *The Future of the Earth*, Harry N. Abrams, 2004

Morgan, Sally, *Waste, Recycling and Reuse* (Sustainable Futures), Evans Brothers Ltd., 2005

Spilsbury, Louise, *A Sustainable Future: Saving and Recycling Resources* (Geography Focus), Heinemann Library, 2006

Ganeri, Anita, *Woodlands and Forests in Danger* (Protecting Habitats), Franklin Watts, 2008

Glossary

afforestation planting trees where none previously grew.

agroforestry an efficient way of growing crops within a forest area. Trees may be thinned out but not cleared completely.

Amazon Basin a major rainforest region in South America, including much of Brazil, Peru and Colombia.

biodiversity an ecosystem with a wide range of species. Any exploitation of the ecosystem does not reduce the number of plants, insects, wildlife and fungi in the area.

biome a global-scale ecosystem, covering a large area, with a distinct variation of species within it.

canopy the upper layer of a rainforest, in which the tops of the trees merge together to keep the sunlight out.

carbon store all vegetation contains carbon, building up reserves as plants grow and releasing them slowly back into the environment after death. Rapid destruction like burning releases all the carbon quickly, as in the case of rainforest burning.

cash crops crops grown for sale rather than for the use of the farmers themselves. Usually they are grown on large plantations and consist of a single crop type.

clearance deforestation of a large area of forest for exploitation, either of the timber itself or to use the land for another purpose, such as agriculture.

deforestation cutting timber in an area unsustainably, so that large areas of forest are destroyed.

desertification either the spreading of a desert into its adjacent areas, or the change of a previously non-desert area into a desert, due to changes in climate and vegetation. These changes may be natural or the result of human activity.

ecosystem a community of living plants, animals, insects and the environment in which they live.

erosion the wearing away of soil or rocks by natural processes such as wind or water.

global warming the rise in global temperatures that is causing climate change. Forest destruction seems to speed up global warming. When it happens naturally, change is slow. If human activity is the cause, the speed of change is much faster and it is almost impossible to manage.

green waste dead plant material from many sources, including farms and gardens as well as timber waste, which can be recycled for use as a soil improver and fertiliser.

ground cover small plants growing on the forest floor. In the rainforest they are shade-lovers, as little sunlight penetrates the mass of vegetation above.

groynes lines of timber posts, or fence-like structures along a beach at right angles to the coastline to prevent longshore drift – the process by which waves move beach material along the shore.

hardwood slow-growing trees, deciduous in temperate climates, ideal for furniture and construction. Most trees that grow in the rainforests are hardwoods.

LEDCs less economically developed country – one of the poorer countries of the world. LEDCs include all of Africa, Asia (except Japan), Latin America and the Caribbean, and Melanesia, Micronesia and Polynesia.

logging cutting timber on a large scale. It can be controlled and sustainable, but has more often been highly destructive of forests.

MEDC more economically developed country – one of the richer countries of the world. MEDCs include all of Europe, northern America, Australia, New Zealand and Japan.

mulch a substance usually made from decomposed plant matter, spread over soil to prevent loss of moisture and to act as a fertiliser.

plantation an area where a single tree or bush crop is grown on a large scale. Sun-grown coffee is an example, as rainforest has been cleared and the coffee bushes grow in full sun, without any shade trees. This is a contrast to shade-grown coffee.

pulp a material in the process of turning wood into paper. Some timber-producing countries take the process this far and then export the pulp, which is then made into different types of paper in the importing countries.

re-afforestation replanting trees in an area where the previous woodland has been cut down. Done well, this can be truly sustainable.

revetments wooden slatting, placed at an angle at the base of a cliff to prevent coastal erosion.

shade-grown crops crops produced from bushes and small trees that grow well in the shade of taller trees. This is a sustainable system of producing food and cash crops without damaging the rainforest. Coffee and cocoa are two examples of shade-grown crops.

silt a fine sediment, often of mud or clay, found at the bottom of rivers or lakes. In some circumstances, this sediment can build up so much that it blocks rivers, preventing their flow.

SIP Structured Insulated Panel, i.e. insulation is built into flooring and wall panels made in the factory for construction on a building site.

slash and burn a simple, traditional subsistence method of farming crops in rainforests, involving clearance of trees, burning, hoeing, planting and harvesting.

softwood timber from conifers, mainly used to make furniture, pulp and paper. Usually these trees are quite fast-growing.

soya a bean, high in protein, which is grown for human and animal food. Demand for meat means that more animal fodder is needed. In the Amazon rainforest huge areas have been cut down for soya production.

sustainability exploitation of forests so that the present generation can have what they need without damaging the supply of resources for future generations.

tree nursery a place where seeds and seedlings are cultivated for replanting, to balance the consequences of forest clearance or exploitation.

wood pellets compacted waste wood used a fuel in wood-burning stoves.

Index